LOVE
DREAM
WITH
TELEVISION

HANNAH ENSOR

Book Cover Design: Natalie Eilbert
Book Interior Design: Sarah Gzemski

Published by Noemi Press, Inc. A Nonprofit Literary Organization.
www.noemipress.org.

LOVE
DREAM
WITH
TELEVISION

HANNAH ENSOR

LOVE DREAM WITH TELEVISION: POEMS

MAN/BOY LINE

MAN/BOY LINE

Where is the man/boy line?
When someone refers to the distinction
between liking boys and liking men,
I think, "NAMBLA?"

Sitting on a porch, Maine coast under the moon,
discussing whether or not we were ladies,
I was a boylady. Definitely not

a manlady. Not now a boylady,
but what? Diane, yes, a lady.
Or a woman? People like what
Anne Carson has written

about not being a woman. One time I dated a man
who thought he was a boy while I thought
he was a woman, despite wishing he

were a boy, sometimes being mad
at what a boy he was. He doesn't speak to me now,
but sometimes we park next to each other,
as we work in adjacent buildings.

DESIRE

Artists know how to live! By which I mean,
visual artists know about each other and play

while I sit here in a tiny room. Ross Gay
in an essay about Hazel Meyer: *As she*

would say to me by way of enthusiasm for a project
I have in mind, 'Yes, yes, that's the reason

to be an artist, isn't it? To make art
out of what we want to do and think about?' Crimson

and motherfucking clover. What do I want to do?
Watch the Australian women's team

play basketball. Think about stopped action,
the pause in the game, the overlap between

enlightenment painting and basketball officiating.
Whatever Jeff Van Gundy hates

I want to talk about.
Visual artists have each other, at least.

My first four lines are always practice.
Someone asked Allen Iverson recently, again,

about practice. A chance to clarify
or double down. He did a third thing

that's actually both. I have a question
I can't ask google: Is there consensus

among critics as to which medium
creates the most distance*?

1)   photography
2)   film/cinema
3)   television
4)   painting and the other material arts

.

*And to remind us all, endless distance = desire.

HAREM

I live in endless theorem. I live
relentless correction.
You didn't tell me
we could sell the art:
fiscal touching, fiscal touching
in the courtyard. It elicits
a response. Looking around the house
peeling the wallpaper off,
all so salable. Watch Hardcore Pawn
and sleep. It seems
that death is very possible.
I count my corporeal feelings.
Live peerless. Here-less and there-
less. Here, this: before it's all gone
we should touch the walls,
illicit. Before I gray my hair.
Before I marble statue. As my
grandmother says, Not goodbye
but see you later.

ON TELEVISION IN POEMS

if I write a poem with TELEVISION
in mind but don't SAY IT
or if I just CAST IT DIFFERENTLY
I may make SUCCESSFUL ART
one that creates IN THE MIND OF MY READER
A PLEASURE

if for example I make you A DRAWING
and that drawing is OF FACES
faces I have drawn
and if they otherwise match YOUR DESIRE
for what ART THAT IS MADE OF FACES
looks like
what does it CHANGE:
my caption explaining
"these are faces from DAWSON'S CREEK
season 05 EPISODE 03"
I still love you
this is still a love gesture THIS ONE RIGHT HERE

see, though,
I got you
because IN THAT LAST POEM
there was no "YOU"
the "you" was MADE UP
or it was YOU, THE READER,
until I said "I STILL LOVE YOU"
you did not think THAT I LOVED YOU
but you liked it better
that way, right? I'LL ADMIT IT:
I DID TOO
we want our poems TO HAVE BELOVEDS
because BELOVEDS
give us an excuse TO TALK ABOUT TELEVISION

EVERYONE WANTS AN IMMERSIVE EXPERIENCE

Nature poem at a screening of Jurassic Park

Wendy told me Michael Crichton's a monster.
We look up when he died, and it says *World's
most famous climate denier dies.* 2004.
What a different year. I can't

keep saying these things. As we were driving
to the screening, Aisha humming the theme song, I knew
where all the cymbals crashed. I must
have practiced this before, somewhere
in the deep past of my body.
They show the Prince, George Michael,

David Bowie sing-along preview. Some chuckles.
Some audible sadness. *They all died,* says the woman
in front of me. How do you describe it. The movie starts

with forest sounds and the cosmos. A Universal Studios
joint. The man who appears is Indiana Jones minus the Harrison Ford.
Wondering what we consider success. Not this,
that's for sure. They start out

mining. How likely, mining. There's
amber. *You are alive when they stop to eat you,* the man says.
Everybody wants the science; nobody wants

to pay for it. There are certain songs, certain shades
of green, that make a person feel hope. It's science. I could spend all day

transforming the discourse
into smear campaigns. *We shouldn't be here.* Foreshadowing
and a pair of jeeps. A slow & clumsy removing of one's glasses.
A jaw agape, long neck, strings.
Strings again.
I should take up the viola. To know something well. Everyone's
weak in the knees

at this first sight of dinosaurs and I'm
tearing up too. Maybe I
miss water, or maybe
I'm re-finding my heart. These guys

are scientists, know
what they're talking about. In the 90s,
we used to hear about cloning all the time.
Those sheep. Stefan Urquelle. That one lady's dog.

As in nature, we laugh at lawyers,
hold eggs gingerly. As in nature,
we want a longer look, but the ride keeps moving.

Life finds a way. Goldblum might be getting off
on lesbian dinosaurs. It's not immediately clear.

A grid, a web of scenarios, projectors overlapping
over their heads. *Nature selected them for extinction.*

Is the condor/deforestation/extinct ecosystem storyline

from the mind of Crichton, or is that Big Hollywood?
What year is it again? Nature
makes people differently fertile, differently

ready for children—not to be one but to have one.
We run ourselves thin

on electric tracks. *Hey look!*
Hey look. Nature spares
no cost. In nature,

sound is diffuse. In this theater, we are all disappointed
in that goat.

When you play cymbals in an outdoor situation,
you must open them up and out, you must turn them
to face the audience, the listeners. In nature,
sound dissipates, doesn't stay safe.

Laura Dern wants Timmy to stay safe.
Laura Dern calls an ill stegosaurus *babygirl*.
Nature's majestic waves are crashing. We are off

the coast of Costa Rica. In school, I read
about the sublime. Went to an amusement park.
Heard someone suggest a link between Ansel Adams
and porn. If only they'd seen

this movie. Nature is destructive, as we are
in nature. If there's anything to notice about straight men
in nature, in this movie, it's that they love
but are not good at women. As in nature,

I find it alarming when all the doors unlock and then
lock again. I find it alarming when, suddenly, a goat.

The goat is here to remind you of the hunt.

We sometimes have to remind each other
not to scare ourselves. The glasses of water are there
to remind you of chaos. The authority

is man doctor. Nature is omniscient storytelling,
is third person plural. Is second person:
you, Nature Is the intractability of Seinfeld's Newman,
Pulp Fiction, Laura Dern. Movies work because we've forgotten

that even when someone is an antagonist
we're not supposed to be happy
when they die. A Ford Explorer

in a tree represents possibility. A man
climbing a tree in a movie is not a pastoral.
A young boy who has gone already from Timmy to Tim.

An Explorer in a tree is potential. If you remember
from school: potential energy, that drop. Growing up,

I was told that some Jews don't climb trees.

Some Jews don't buy Fords,
don't play falling games,
or watch action thrillers.

I understand it. Something you might not know about me
is, I love the *Scream* trilogy, my favorite genre
is metafictional television/cinema.
I'm a real sucker for it.

She's yelling *"Alan"* now. At a certain point,
I guess you stop worrying about littering;
somewhere around the gasping for air
loss of your beloved.

The water is a leitmotif. Like me,
Goldblum is a Jew, which makes him perfect
for this moment.

Must go faster—

A movie that presages its own videogame:
this is nature. The moments of calm are the ones
in which we can access aesthetic pleasure,

e.g. the brachiosaurs singing.
These are not-monsters, they are animals now,
they are *doing what they do.*

Cut to the gift shop where there are literal lunch boxes,
a billionaire eating.
It's only this far in that I hear him as Scottish.
I just thought he was rich.
I too am Scottish but don't think of it as my nature.
But you can't think through this one, John, you have to feel it.
The man needs to feed the tree to the animal,

even though the animal was doing just fine:
plenty of tree.

The last time we thought "cow," it was being fed
to a raptor. Movies work because babies are cute
and also terrifying. As in nature.
Footprints stand for babies and for awe
standing for birth leading to death, destruction:

I can't wait anymore.

So many people
have to die.
This is how movies work.
This is how nature works.
Clever girl. This is nature,

and just because you're back inside doesn't mean

you're safe. That's called irony: when the audience watches
a dinosaur open a door. Ellie doesn't know

they can do that. Laura Dern might know: that's
irony, too. When the actors know what the characters
can't: acting. Two siblings trying to save each other
within an industrial fridge: we're getting close now,
close to a finish. We are a movie
that speeds up at the end:

      Old bones
It is our spine crashing down
on us

We are all the decision to, or not to, have children,
We are all deus ex machina saved by a T-Rex,
We are all cranes flying over the ocean,
We are all stocking up on Plan B to prevent this from happening,
We are all a seven-year-old boy at a 10:00 PM screening of Jurassic
Park, and the movie is over.

Everyone claps, cute and weird, for whom, and we go outside.
Outside, where we are all a half-moon, bottom-heavy, after the movie,
trying hard not to get hit by cars.

SPECTACULAR 01: SUPER BOWL XLVIII

Tom Brady looks angry and the game
hasn't even started. His wife

asked us all to pray for him, pray   for Tom.   There she is
in a special box, we can
barely see her: just enough to know that she

is the model who married
Tom Brady.   Please, God, let Tom Brady win
another Super Bowl!   Gisele asked us
to pray. Half the game
goes by; the football players stop playing

and Madonna dances. She is
fifty-three years old. There are exaggerated feathers

and soldiers, and she wears gold lamé.   The lamé is gone
but we don't get to see   how.   Soldiers swing swords,
and the football field

melts into Madonna   who is fifty-three   a cheerleader.
Nicki Minaj and M.I.A. and Cee-lo Green

are there. I've heard one of them
is racist, one of them thinks rape is okay. The things we think
we know   about other people.   I swear I had this dream

once   but it was Nanci Griffith
not Madonna and Madonna is fifty-three years old says

this is just like a prayer   yes   I myself
prayed for it, and   when she evaporates into a cloud of smoke
only the stage

is left, and it says WORLD PEACE

EVERY TACTIC IS STILL GIRL

For a moment I wonder:
What referential? What gerund (e.g. "emailing")
centers its own habit? A voicemail
on my work line, someone
can't reach his son. I'm prompted
to re-enter my code. I'm not sure
"girl" is the right tack after all.
My passphrase ends with a comma.
There is a girl for every visual referent,
a right tack and a left one.
I keep using words as if I know
what they mean. I want my thoughts
to refuse their own habit energy,
but then it would not be habit.

NEW YEAR POEMS, 2016

New Year Poem 1

deep in the pocket
of the Univ. system, I'm
right where they want me
on the verge of no money
and too lucky to leave
rich dad poor dad
or to quote a friend of mine
ARTS ADMIN IS FOR WIVES

1-2-16 Poem

Everyone's got a New Year's poem
Everyone's got a desert plants in Tucson poem
Everyone's got their David standing by the lake
taking his shirt off poem. I wouldn't write it
if it didn't arouse me, is what all the poets say.
I've written enough of these to stop
before I've even really begun because I know
this one's gonna be bad too. Every set of details
as sad as the last. I bought that CD
with my cousin in Boston years
ago and the lyrics said it best: "It doesn't even matter."

Back to Work Poem 1-5-16

Clouds in the sky. In a painting. Now your new
Bluetooth headphones—your big announcement. That's a magic rub.
Two people have congratulated me. I brought coffee and
Toblerone. DVDs to mail. Panes and panes of glass, a goodbye
or two. There's a delightful human under here.

METABOLISM

Pressing on my thumbnail to check capillary
response I am a dumb mess with information
and fear well I "come by it honestly" my mom
would say I now agree in ways she wouldn't like
and ditto for how I disagree I'm not in
a "3G" group for third generation survivors
of the Shoah I am perfectly glad with how
hard that work is for me and in my body
when I go to the local Holocaust museum I need
days of nothing after I need to be alone this
is how I want it I do not want more
or less of any of it I have a slow
metabolism take what my DO considers
placebo levels of all my pills and when I say
here are the four things I want to talk about
she says let's talk first about your anxiety

GRAND CANYON DEATH OPTIONS

1   condor swoops picks you up drops you directly in the middle of the thing directly over where the river is, the canyon is your radius, the rim, and you drop and drop into it

2   unexpected weather, unexpected wind gust, pushes your body (which is a wind shield, a land sail) into the canyon from the rim: tumble tumble it is unexpected

3   your lover photographs you then pushes you in

4   your lover throws your sandwich or Wallace Stevens book or grandmother or water bottle over the edge and you run after it, you have made your choice

5   jump! as far forward as you can (which is at most in the tens of feet you are no olympian and even if you were)

6   you somewhat desire water (though "desire" is perhaps too strong a word for what you feel) and it seems that the closest water is that river at the bottom so you say "be right back" and start climbing—or walking and climbing— down toward the river neither totally comprehending nor caring how long that will take you (numbers and warnings mean nothing) and you die wearing jeans and a baseball cap somewhere just a few miles into your half-hearted trek

7   condor shadow makes everything dark then again bright and a seizure disorder you didn't know you had sends you wildly flailing into the largesse; the cavern; the expanse; and down you go wild and yourself expansive beyond any previous expectation you had regarding your frail human limits and above you the condor shits, shits freely, for there has never been and never will be any reason not to

8   not enough water

9   there is snow packed and matted at the edge; you slip and
     it seems so obvious

10   your lover does not yet want to share the milky way bar
     you brought to the canyon and so, feeling fat, you throw
     yourself over the edge

11   some bird you think you have seen before but you have
     actually never seen before hops toward you and again
     toward you and something about being given an
     opportunity seems to scream out to you it is a voice that
     commands do not move no sudden movements and so the
     bird (it is blue) continues hopping toward you until it is at
     your feet and it hops atop one of your feet and slowly slowly
     you reach out and touch its head so lightly and it
     flies away and three months later you die of unexplained
     causes

12   (in this option you are the bird) a person who wants to
     reckon with mortality (his/her own) and scale (in this you
     are implicated) throws a rock or a branch or a plastic bottle
     cap as far as he/she can (not very far; see death option 5)
     and on its way down this projectile hits you squarely on
     the head, it is certainly not enough force to kill or injure
     you but you are confused, it is fairly stunning and
     unexpected, and in your confusion you fly into the edge of
     the canyon and tumble down already dead

13   you and your lover survive your trip to the canyon without
     impulsively pushing one another into it; you are in the car
     and you leave the park watching the sun set over yet
     another set of desert canyons; once you arrive home you
     take off your boots and your socks and your thin spring
     coats; you begin pushing each other to the ground because
     you can, because it is safe now, because the wood floor
     will certainly hold, stay where it is, will certainly not
     collapse into a crevasse a mile deep, because there are no
     more mules or condors or strangers with cameras; you
     take turns pushing and pushing and pushing each other

over until it is the middle of the night and you are both exhausted and bruised and crying on the floor; you close your eyes and think of the forests you drove through today; you fall asleep safe on the floor; still and someday you will die.

SPECTACULAR 02: SINGLE LADIES (PUT A RING ON IT)

At some point, it stops being real: the room, the time, our eyes. Beyoncé's still dancing, but suddenly, it's like I'm tripping and she's not.   Out of breath: I could never love you as much as I love "Single Ladies (Put a Ring On It)." I could never be bionic. What is a woman: Human.   Her smile.   Her metal hand.   Love begets love. Thighs on a screen just killing me. This music video, I have paid for it. It is and it is not forever. Beyoncé, the woman, the real person, once danced, wearing exactly that, in a real room. I heard her say in an interview   that her mom made the leotards the night before. In the real room, there were two other women dancing; there was a flashbulb in the real room. There was someone, if not someones, operating a or some camera(s). I look at her eyes. Mascara. Leotard. There is a moment for look-ing at   seeing   thighs. Monochrome, Beyoncé: these are death sentences, and I am shattered I am shattered by this screen.

SPECTACULAR 03: JENNY SCHECTER

When Jenny first moves to LA, she doesn't know she's going to be a lesbian, but that's what happens. We kind of know it's where her life is headed, what with the stolen glances and the fact that she's the main character of a show called *The L Word*. Everyone who watches *The L Word* is happy when she makes out with Marina, who is foreign and reads Anne Carson and has dark hair and a café. Poor Tim, though. He starts out the show engaged: engaged to Jenny: Jenny who's a lesbian. There's not really anything wrong with him, it's Jenny who's to blame. Tim, though: he's a swim instructor, handsome, a good man.

DENNIS RODMAN HAS ME ALL CONFUSED

For what it's worth I've read more books and articles about masculinity than anything else

Sometime around October 2016 my partner said, "Dennis Rodman has me all confused," and we both laughed,

because she meant Donald Trump,
and it was October 2016

Dennis Rodman famous for wedding dress
famous for hair and almost-horizontal rebounds
famous for his friendship with Kim Jong Il

Remember when it used to be funny and weird but largely unworrisome that Dennis Rodman went to North Korea

I gave a guest lecture on Holocaust poetry once and talked about contemporary Jewish poets and legacies of trauma, indirect influence, influence not of events but of epigenetics

that was 2015

These days most of the things I read are about a president seemingly no one wants
I don't know anyone
who wants this president, but I read about him constantly

The podcasts I listen to in August 2017 come with disclaimers that the world might have changed since they recorded

might have changed drastically

if you are checking the dates of these poems, I would request you do so not as a historian, but as a forensic psychologist, the kind you've seen on TV,

not necessarily for what has already happened but for what
those things having happened
has done to us

NATURE POEM WHILE WATCHING JURASSIC PARK

Every introductory class begins with a big question, e.g. *What is Nature?*

Every television show begins with a big tension, one that ranges from easily-resolvable to one that makes viewers uncomfortable. Depending on the show it may also begin with a joke, a recognizable theme song or ditty.

Every day begins with some variation of light. I'm trying to start my day slower, with fewer screens from the onset. More natural light.

What is nature? 30% of our brains and sometimes 66% of our brain activity is visual. This is why I have to close my eyes to calm down. One thing I know is that I would watch the sunset for hours if I could. What is a sunset, anyway?

If I were a character in Jurassic Park, I might monologue thusly: *I am frustrated with all of the ways that the world around me functions. If only it wouldn't; if only we could. I can only be so much to you. You, nature.*

A friend of mine took an intro class in neurobiology. I was helping her study and a flashcard told me that a very high percentage of our memories—70%?—are constructed. I still bring it up when I see her. Our fears distort our reality.

I am working on a taxonomy though I am not sure what the object, what the subject.

It would be easy to start any class like this. Ask students to spin around a question, almost too big. It is an object on a wheel and you know it is unstable. You like watching things wobble and it has a certain effect. We call this "manipulative," we call this "pedagogy." There are power dynamics in a classroom, often confused with eros. Watching things wobble can be called "flirtation."

Many movies work because of romantic love. Goldblum flirts with Dern even while she yells "Alan." Laura Dern, intractable, was the reason Ellen's character came out twenty years ago. She didn't work for years after that, Dern. What is nature? Is it a place

where people fall in love? Who are those people? Did they pay an entry fee to nature? What percentage of our brain activity is occupied while we are falling in love? What is my problem, and what can I do with it?

I am thirty-one years old and would either be very good at school or just lousy. I would either make a good character in this movie or I would be dead. Some things you hear over and over again and only years later do you realize you never stored them away in a way you can do anything with.

One time I attended a seminar. It was a three- or four-hundred level one, asked with its tongue in its cheek, Is Nature White? And then we sat around waiting for *Black Nature* to come out. Why did we wait? What is memory? What is a sunset? Which are we more likely to see? What is a question that is good, and what makes that question good? The sun set hours ago. I didn't see it. I'm not sure I even thought of it as it was happening.

ON ART IN POEMS

"Looking at things does give us visual pleasure."
– Paul Ivey

A single-camera mode of production is one distance:
a deference to system or symbol of the artist itself, the artist in
situ:

We watch the sitcom from home (I use "we"

loosely): <u>Man and Task</u> a painting I saw
laughed aloud alongside of

for hours   every time it comes to mind: laugh again.

Jonathan Borofsky

made a big stack of papers with numbers on it.

Who even knows what we'll do   about television
I use "we"   loosely Borofsky

wrote all of the numbers
from 1 to 3227146

was writing numbers
from 1969 to 1986
it wasn't   a lifetime, & it also wasn't lifeless nudes

as a perfectly formal activity. If we're getting formal,

Alex Katz is a man. All of Alex

is man. I haven't been to an art museum in ages,
not in any way
I could enjoy I'm starting   to understand

all my neuroses are
one neurosis: all my neurosis.

I'm on my way to the museum.
Really I'd like to see a film that gets longer at the end.

I keep trying and trying but my painter friends don't like this work
very much.

ON INSTANT REPLAY

Largely due to the "linguistic turn" that has dominated the humanities since the mid-twentieth century, many contemporary scholars and artists habitually equate works of art with highly coded texts to be deciphered, deconstructed, or otherwise interpreted.

– Jorella Andrews and Simon O'Sullivan

Beginning with the 2014-15 NBA regular season, the NBA will launch its new state-of-the-art NBA Replay Center, based in Secaucus, N.J. The NBA Replay Center will be fueled by a groundbreaking high-speed arena network to enhance the performance of NBA referees and to accelerate the replay review process.

– NBA.com

An experiment: instant replay as aesthetic tableau, affect. Is it possible to look at it without assessing, to interrupt that suggested purpose and patterning? So far no. So far I can't imagine it. Claudia Rankine slowed down to the frame the Zidane replay. A head butt sustained over time. Click (pause) click (pause) click (pause) click toward the inevitable, the lyric content moving over slowly. We know how it will end. Jane Miller says poetry is about time. Or she said it's not. Basketball is about time. Tick (pause) tick (pause) tick (pause) tick how many actions on average till a clock expires. The clock the thing that determines the outcome more than any other single factor. Time axial in a way that ball passing through hoop is not. A basketball game could theoretically transpire without a single occurrence of a ball passing through a hoop (think: goaltending). The duration closes, elapses, and then it is decided. What does the clock have to do with our affective possibilities?

What does the time spent on a replay—conferring with Secaucus—around a monitor—must we watch them watch the same footage we watch they watch in Secaucus—do to us? For one the commentators bemoan how long it takes, when they've already reached conclusions of their own. The fans at home turn to Twitter. Refresh (read) refresh their feeds. I do not mean to be dramatic when I suggest that the slowing of action is dangerous because it reminds us of death. What are we doing here. Why am I watching this. That's what the commentators mean when they say it's "bad for the game." What do they say in Secaucus? Have we not yet entirely perished?

As real a question: can I look at a replay—one played on constant repeat for the duration of the official review to determine if that set of motions constitutes (three possible options) a common foul, a flagrant 1, a flagrant 2—as if it is a mural, a poem. As if it is an object not to be read but to be, to affect [us] [or intrans.]. What does that flower mean, nobody ever asks. What does that poem mean, nobody will ever ask again. What does that elbow catapulting into groin mean. Is there a fourth option, when I watch this replay. Not in this moment relevant: the category of foul. Any foul at all. Any categories at all. What do I see in the bodies moving into and around each other. Would be too easy to say the erotic. Would be too easy to say sexy sinew or conflict or desire or sweat, too narrative still. When practicing with blind contour we are encouraged to instruct the eye not to call a thing tomato, leaf. But to follow the curve, edge, line. Can I do this here. When calling up a memory of a replay rather than interrogating an image fresh. Even "interrogating" a problem to be released. A clenched muscle. It has already congealed into interpreted data. I call that memorized shape James Harden. I call that memorized shape Ball. Beard. Elbow. Half court. Intention, happenstance, intercepting bodies. A "natural" or an "unnatural" act. One of many questions. Limited by the genre. Red. Uniform. It is step one to recognize that a muscle is clenched. To feel it clench. Do not yet worry about releasing, adjusting. Okay, now relax. See if you can relax.

ART IN A CAPITALISM

People in other countries are also interested in toothbrush
deodorant wine reception. Not all art affects its viewer
universally, but walking into a gallery does do something to a
person, or should I say to me.

Talking over lunch to piped-in Motown discussing O'Hara's "I do
this I do that." Through jetlag I paraphrase: "I see this I say that."
1000 króna

to enter the small photography museum: it's ok. In a book outside
the gallery, the spine cracks a little when I turn the pages, I turn
them to find photos of women bent uniformly

to clean the steps. The book is new, large format, bad glue, I
might be the first to open it. New book, old photos; it's 2017. I
don't know who even cares anymore if the steps are clean.

ACUPUNCTURE

What might have happened if, instead of dropping out of the music school, I had gone to acupuncture?

Sometimes I drop back into a past body just long enough for it to become a dream body

If I dream it hard enough, Jeff is there again on the floor while I practice marimba in a grey boring room

Just marimba, soundproofing, shitty carpet, mirror, Jeff. Not really knowing what I was doing there (or is that a later me, looking back and saying "young")

I like to notice things, and this too keeps me from relaxing

Earlier today I was noticing too much too

Indiscriminately and not at all usefully

I spent some time noticing things about people

And about the needle between but above my eyes

The two sticking well into my trapezius

How many times the acupuncturist dabbed at my forehead after removing the needle

I was needless, or it was needless, all of it

All this noticing and still no yield

What is it I expect of life

Of a day or of myself

ANOTHER STORY ABOUT THE MAN/BOY LINE

And on what side of it
I am

a note stuck to a wall in an office
is not an endorsement

For days I wear the same
shorts

Do not anymore
want to strap it on

A partner I loved left me because
I did not know enough

about myself

POETRY IS NOT ABOUT MEMORY: FOR JEFF

Fish and chips in Canada.   Malt vinegar.   As a child.   A very
different border.   Some car   maybe another.   Definitely
father.   The curly-haired one   who is still alive.   If later I read
that sentence   . I will cry.   Another memory   I will make will
involve flowers;   I will probably   order them.   Did you know
that twenty-eight year olds   too can die? I   have a friend who
was twenty-eight   and now   isn't. And a friend   who was
twenty-eight   and is now a widow.   That funeral   was today
in Michigan.   Michigan to Canada, a short   trip. I have always
been afraid   of authority figures.   They make me cry so easily.
A bike cop has,   border official,   tall booming-voiced band
director.   I guess I did   break his xylophone.   Jeff was there
too.   Now that I'm older   I know that things   cost money.
The band director   is retired   but still alive.   My father   is
still   alive. His mother is   too   which every day   amazes
me. She is   Canadian. Or,   I guess,   Scottish.   American?
Canadians love   vinegar. When we put it on   French fries   we
are saying something   about Canada. Maybe something   to
Canada or to   ourselves.   I went to Canada a few times   as
a child.   Besides the vinegar,   there were also   casinos, some
locks   and a bridge.

AN AQUEDUCT

In a sense
this is my doing:

a tent erect
and shedding
its walls. A creek
we're down it

without regret. At least I asked.

At least I pushed the canoe. Pushed it back,
insolvent. Speaking of ugly,

night is approaching.
Speaking of night, *come on*.

When the waves crash at the seacoast it is
a little hello how are you.
A small hug. It disrupts

the sunset. It interrupts the radio:
"Love is a Battlefield."

I wrote a psalm:

> *little roman boys*
> *aqueduct*

Though, what is a psalm? 4–3–4–3 is a hymn, love *is*
a battlefield and in it we stay
and erect structures

menstruate

WITH A HEAVY HEART

Isaiah Thomas is playing today
without his sister

His sister who died
yesterday in a car

her name
sharpied onto his shoes

The commentators
are obsessed

We've been pathologized
I mean pathos-ized
We just watch the replay of him crying

no sister

on the sidelines
he is
"the best point guard in the eastern conference"
Chuck says John Wall is
Ernie says really
Ernie says better than IT?
I think Better than Kyrie? there are
plenty of good basketball
players

in the eastern conference

how many
    have sisters

IN THE 90s MY PERCEPTIONS OF POPULAR CULTURE GOT ALL MUDDIED UP WITH SHAME, GENERALIZED CONFUSION, AND ANXIETY.

"Not a complaint."
– Anne Carson

Disney characters are mostly naked. It is nothing anti-lesbian as I'd once contrived. It has almost nothing to do with me, in fact. I'm not a Carrie or a Samantha

but a young Simba. When I was young, I hated Stevie Nicks because of a feeling in my chest, ditto that 4 Non Blondes song that played at all of the b'nei mitzvot.

Re-reading Wallace Stevens, it occurs to me that historically much of philosophy has been bare

masculine narcissism. Not necessarily a complaint. My poems too are about me, but hopefully they   Well, I'm not sure what I hope. When I was nine years old or so,

my friend Rachel and I wrote fan letters to Jonathan Taylor Thomas. He wrote back to her but not to me.   This is not my root: confusing identity with desire.   I am

sitting next to a number of toy figurines in a bookstore. The ones I'm drawn to: Simba, Aladdin, bunny with tall ears. Not drawn to: all of the others.

GREEN AVENTURINE RELEASES OLD PATTERNS, HABITS, AND DISAPPOINTMENTS SO NEW GROWTH CAN TAKE PLACE.

When Chance says "fucked all
my friends" is that a queer

statement   is it communist

"that old adage and historical
tragedy: communism is better
than communists"

To my left on the plane,
a teen, I almost say,
"you're not Lonzo Ball"

teenage / skinny / strong
legs spiked at a 45-degree angle

replace queer with femme
replace adidas snap pants with

this year, 2017
and me   fresh-shorn on a plane

to Iceland Aventurine around
my neck

          / a revolution / we

have to be revolutionaries
not just at the end of the quarter / no

all the time / when we first wake up
and thereafter

SISTER SCORER, RIVULET

"She's been looking to be more of a facilitator and a sister here in this second half. She needs to be a scorer."
— Rebecca Lobo commenting on Game 5, 2016 WNBA playoffs

What does it mean
to be   sister
in sport

To   sister sport   here with 2:49 to go

            wandering through a gallery
the other day

I found myself not lingering
in front of vulvar art
        by a cisman

In art,
I think you must sister   the vulva

In my home,
I hear footsteps, a WNBA game,
dogs barking

I am
still   a sister rivulet

a game   a month

WATCHING THE NBA PLAYOFFS, SUMMER IN TUCSON

San Antonio Spurs vs. Oklahoma City Thunder; May 2, 2016
Game 2, Conference Semi-Finals
In which the Thunder tie the series at one win a piece

Is it just me or do the commentators say fewer fucked up things these days? I used to watch basketball and just be pissed. I can barely remember why. It's possible that I've settled into my old age, an atrophy. I bought an issue of Art in America with a painting of two flattened basketballs growing out of flattened flowers against a matte black backdrop. I'm streaming Spurs-Thunder on *TNT Overtime*. How many years ago was it that I was writing to my then-boyfriend about driving across the country with my dad trying to find a livestream of the Playoffs. LeBron was still in Miami and ended up winning it all. In the arena and through TV: they play "Don't Stop Believing." Why don't live DJs do this? I'm sure they'd be willing to be part of the 1099 economy I'm hearing so much about. Everyone wants the songs, no one wants to pay for them. Danny Green is reprising his 2013 Finals performance, the one thing people know him for. Lots of unexpected threes. Impossible by definition to repeat but he can echo. On *TNT Overtime* instead of commercials you get to see the arena when the action stops, the TV broadcast otherwise at commercial. During these pauses the commentators don't say anything. Then they come back in after not saying a word for up to three minutes. I like to imagine they have stopped talking entirely   have spent some time quiet   but it's more likely that producers have muted their lavalier microphones. If the ball hits a spectator's leg, that is out of bounds. I go full screen. I try to like Kawhi Leonard but don't yet. It's a one-point game. I never don't like the Oklahoma City Thunder. It is summer in Tucson, and I wear a lot of tank tops while watching basketball. I can't imagine my shoulders that broad. Even the guys I think of as sleek, small, quick: they've got shoulders. This pause gives me a chance to read "COLLISON" through a transparent white warmup shirt. I don't think it's left his shoulders this whole game.

THE ANXIETY OF RESPONSIBLE MEN

A picture of a longdead poet smiling sweetly at a small child. Two smiles, they kill me from beyond the grave. I'm not worried anymore about what photography isn't or does in society (death). So many thoughts abandoned. They rise to the surface at surprising moments, the blackberries in a Kinnell poem: unbidden. I understand that whoever you read in your 200-level poetry class becomes the canon. You assume everyone else too has read that poem: it's standard issue. I find it hard not to be nasty when I suggest that maybe it shouldn't be so. It's hard to disentangle feeling from it. Objectivity is a male feature. Making clouds into items. Even that feels too metaphorical, too **** *******. It's hard not to be nasty. The best fact that I can get to at the moment involves the online thing for your W-2. Objectivity

is a male feature, we are made to aspire to it. We are made to aspire toward not anymore feeling the minor sensations as major. "You are the only way I can be in a statement." I'm such a Libra. And you are a scholar of the sexual grouping, a practitioner of what you do with your own body. And maybe what others do with theirs, next to yours. Miley Cyrus, Caitlyn Jenner, and Helena Peabody's mom have all made the news lately as women with bodies. You, though, you feel like an encasement. Textbooks making easy work of spaces, shapes, spirals. This, I could quit. This, an encasement. Am I using it right? How embarrassing! As if I just learned of this category. When I was young I did not understand that I was already serious. Now I understand and can only vaguely do anything with that information except point back at what I made and say, *See?* I'm such a Libra. Libras are co-dependent. I am a literal body

so sick of nonbooks put forth by male survivors of male artists who died but these male survivors have presses and they make us pay twenty-four dollars for a terrible book with expensive cover design, they dupe us into caring about the dead male and buying his book that was never a book while he lived, which is certainly not to suggest that worthwhile art is only ever published while the worthwhile artist is still alive, but instead that we are encouraged to read a twenty-four dollar posthumous book with some kind of relish, that some types of dead people are intended to persist past their moment of immediate relevance, I could reference particular moments but that would dull my point which is that their point is dull, that

the point of their misogyny is how gentle it is,

so gentle that we applaud, well I know when that Hotline Bling

it can only mean one thing

SPECTACULAR 04: AT THE ROSE GARDEN

There was always something in Portland, like when we went to go see the Trail Blazers play at the Rose Garden and there were strobe lights and indoor blimps all around and they kept teasing prizes, prizes for the crowd, if Portland scored a certain number of points and so we were laughing and filming each other with our phones and yelling GUY DEBORD!! like real assholes and the players I had heard of were playing better than the players I hadn't heard of and by the end of the game the whole crowd was chanting CHA LU PA   CHA LU PA   the whole crowd was chanting and my ears hurt and I was nervous but happy to be there with you and by the time we left the arena my fists were full of coupons I never even considered redeeming.

WATCHING THE NBA PLAYOFFS, SUMMER IN TUCSON

Miami Heat vs. Toronto Raptors; Sunday, May 15, 2016
Game 7, NBA Conference Semi-Finals
In which the Raptors end the Heat's season, Raptors move on, Dwyane Wade's final game in a Miami uniform

It's been so long since I had my period, I've almost forgotten
how to do it. Perfect almond print of blood on khaki shorts
I thought I was just sweating through

Valenciunas is out for his fourth straight game
is there on the sidelines
wearing a camouflage blazer

I'm still drinking my first cup of coffee
it's almost 3:00 PM

>   *I've got no problem with it; now is it dangerous? Absolutely.*

>   (Commentator Mark Jackson, during a foul review)

>   *I once did the same thing to my little brother who passed*
>   *away a few years ago.*

Dwyane Wade's got no one out there.

>   *It may not be a popular decision with the crowd, but I'd*
>   *consider Hack-a-Biyombo right now*

>   (Mark Jackson again)

Leaning over the kitchen counter watching basketball
my back to the dogs / I want to spend more time facing them

a "Hack-a" is an intentional foul to send a bad free-throw shooter to
the line
it is typically a sign of desperation from a strategy perspective
though increasingly coaches
have been choosing to implement it to disrupt momentum

when a free-throw shooter is just that bad, or when they want to
encourage the other team's coach
to take that player out of the game entirely

The Heat chose to foul Biyombo, just like Jackson said, and he
made both shots

Whatever your strategy is, you have to be serious about it
This is now me scolding myself / Like Dwyane Wade, I am alone
this summer

For me the story of this postseason is D-Wade and the
unexpected three

I can't imagine having to sit in a room full of so much joy
You are Dwyane Wade and your eyes a little yellow with tears

He was a huge Heat fan growing up, loved Dwyane Wade

(Commentator Mike Breen, about Raptor Kyle Lowry, who
finished with 35 points, 7 assists)

I'm not a coach and definitely not a player, but I can tell based on
the angle
of the elbow and how close the ball gets to the player's head in
their pre-shot windup
whether or not that one's going in

OTHER PEOPLE

Before anyone in my life had a Kindle Anne Carson had a Kindle
It was her way of reading when in Iceland
I think it was Iceland,
before anyone in my life
went to Iceland

We wouldn't call either thing particularly avant-garde, I don't think
This is why we love Anne Carson

I wonder if one can know so much about art
that it is impossible to make it anymore
Like something breaks, and it is all scattered on the floor
That is too cogent a simile for what I imagine it feeling like

I have long been curious about how Anne Carson feels about
other people

THE ANXIETY OF
RESPONSIBLE MEN

THE ANXIETY OF RESPONSIBLE MEN

for, but not about, Joe Paterno, etc.

(1)

Before any of this came out
we took truth   very seriously

      Now we ask: can we still?   We don't
think so   but it's what we want. We

wander around villages
aflame   we are naked and the heat

gets to us.
                  Yes: the village is on fire

and we are charred.

      Uh oh   you say to me
I'm afraid I might be lying again

(2)

Sitting cross-legged   on the bottom
      of the well, you are not   calling out for help.
You can't   keep calling out

all day   there are certain hours   in which you are sure
there is no one
      nearby

there is no one up there so
            you do not call   This moment you are in

      was preceded by exactly one hour   of not calling out

In the next hour
a squirrel will fall in and join you

(3)

How is a person
supposed to make a plan   to do anything
at all

There is no positive reinforcement

for planning, only the anxiety
of responsible men.   I plan to stay here

for 84, 403, 9, 10, 10, 10, 10,

it doesn't even matter.

There will come a day   when I am
scolded for my failures

asked impolitely   (and I will have earned it)   to leave.

SPECTACULAR 05: RIGHT

I watched an episode of *Law & Order* last night   in which they found a skeleton of someone   assumed dead in the World Trade Center

they had to figure out if the hand and the purse that they'd found at Ground Zero was related to the handless skeleton in Hell's Kitchen and   of course it was   so then they had to figure out if anyone could even prove that this woman had been at work on the day that she was supposedly killed in the World Trade Center and nobody could

the episode hinged on it being   her night purse not her work purse   they'd found at Ground Zero   of course   a lover took it there   before the police had secured the area at 5:00 pm that day, what a useful cover   that 9/11 happened right after he killed his fiancé   At no point are we asked

to consider his first thoughts when the planes hit the towers As soon as the episode ended

I looked at twitter   a conversation with Femi Omoni   who wrote his dissertation on TV policing

ENNOBLING OF THE AMERICAN POLICE THROUGH THE MEDIA

the police lobbied for it   when they felt like TV representation was too   bumbling too cruel not nice enough   a tough combination though

it makes sense   a lot of cruelty passed off as "innocent" "mistakes" these days   HOW COULD HE HAVE POSSIBLY KNOWN BETTER / DONE BETTER I can hear being

said   This morning Aisha and I had a fight

on our way to work after I turned down a street that had two cop cars pointing   their drivers' windows at each other   she asked me to go a different way   I paused   I wasn't even sure there was a different way   thought there wasn't another side street between them and us but then a side street appeared and so I turned down it   Aisha silent for the whole rest of the drive to work both of us thinking to ourselves about Philando Castile but me also   so sure it would've been fine   no question   I wouldn't have turned   if it was just me   and I was thinking too about how I did everything right   so she shouldn't be

mad at me   I grew up watching

Law & Order   comfort viewing   reminds me of falling asleep in my parents' room with my sister there too   all of us   falling asleep

SPEECH ACT

The speech act [that works] here is "I Quit," and I hear myself say it not in the dream version, but in the real one which is me sitting in a yellow chair in the corner ~~thinking through what it means for professional gatekeepers to arbitrate a sphere. How we got there as opposed to a grind.~~

A former professor of mine told us to steal tricks. That was what we were supposed to do as we read. This same professor slept with students, all of whom did not look like me. I'll bet without describing them, you know   what they look like. Contemporary poetics and who gets to decide what's good. It's true I too like *Don't Let Me Be Lonely* most but

the joke that's not a joke is ~~that not everyone is supposed to be the same audience the same reader and also I'm not supposed to be in charge of a book's reception or readership. I don't whisper these things   to people who respect my opinion. As if~~ my upper hand would matter. An underhanded this or that,

a pitch I think. In the meantime no one is tearing down Siken when they think *Crush* is better. I happen to like *War of the Foxes* but

perhaps this is more a regional distinction or one of insider/outsider aesthetics, ~~lyricism and emotion versus art jokes,~~ either of which is on its own a ridiculous binary all binaries now unfortunately mostly connoting ~~Eric or Melania Trump~~ more than the basement art houses of this or that minor city.

META-INTERLUDE; OR, LET'S TAKE A BREAK: A NOTE ON AUDIENCE AND REFERENCE

1.
No one likes to feel stupid.

2.
I have written this book with a very personal set of references. Which is not to say that they are more to me than they are or can be to you. Indeed one of the things I want you to know is that there are no "in jokes" in popular culture. This is how you know it is populist, globalist, social. All the same my body and mind exist in contact with a particular constellation of references, and you with yours. Please do feel free to google along where my references are not yours; feel free to guess and substitute a name. My John Travolta might be your Keanu Reeves on a bench. My LeBron James might be your Milan Kundera. Do, though, scroll through images of "Russell Westbrook postgame outfit" if you have a chance. While some names, sporting activities, or television moments may slip by, I promise that you are as smart, if not smarter, than I am. I happen to think it is easier in our culture to criticize the appearance of popular figures, sporting bodies, e.g. to say "I don't know who Russell Westbrook is or what he is doing in this book" than it is to say "I have not read much Wittgenstein so you should take him out." Both may be true but I ask that you bear with me as I let my constellation be here with us. As a final note, I will mention that some non-lesbians did not care for *Carol*; they thought it was a slow film. Some non-queers and non-women do not see the big deal about Kate McKinnon or the *Lady Ghostbusters* movie. I even heard someone say they didn't get *Moonlight*. If you have not watched *Jurassic Park*, a CNN New Years' Eve special, or a Super Bowl, I want you here in this book with me. Please do feel free to visualize your favorite historical Travolta when I bring him into this with us. He is your Travolta too. This is your biography. This is your U.S. History book. This is your annotated copy of *Our Bodies, Our Selves*.

3.

No one likes to feel stupid. It is a silly thing to fear, but here we all are, doing it anyway. I do believe we are all afraid of feeling stupid, and when we start to feel stupid, we turn this fear into resentment. *I'm not stupid, that's not what I am*, we spit at nothing. But despite the stubbornness of this, we're right: we're not stupid. Stupid is barely even a thing, barely even a possibility. I don't know many people I would describe as "stupid." One time, in college over drinks, I met with a mentor, a literary critic, a highly-regarded professor of mine, and I told her about a meeting I had coming up with another professor. She looked at me over the edge of her vodka and intoned in a low tone, "Not smart." About her colleague, tenured, R1. Not smart. This has stuck with me, perhaps because it is also one of the few moments I have heard someone, a nonstranger at least, accused of this. Usually the people calling other people stupid are missing out on a lot of the work they could be doing on their hearts, their pelvic floor, their third eye. You are not stupid. I am not stupid. When I was in college, around the same time as this professor but theoretically unrelatedly, my therapist told me to subject everything I say to myself to "the friend test": if you wouldn't speak to your friend that way, do not speak to yourself that way. I call myself stupid but I'm not. I call myself stupid, but I would not call my friend stupid; she is not. I call myself stupid but a friend would never call me stupid. What's the difference, then? The difference, in theory, is that my friend loves me, and I love my friend. I think that I love me, but this is not how I talk to people I love. My book loves you, sometimes calls itself stupid. It would be horrified if it knew that you thought that it thought that you were stupid, that it was calling you stupid. It loves you. You are a friend.

ELECTOR DAY IN THE GUEST HOUSE: DECEMBER 19, 2016

I've been reading this article   <https://littlequeerideograms.
wordpress.com/2016/11/14/queer-grief-and-the-secret-
chord-with-kate-mckinnon-its-a-cold-and-its-a-broken-
hallelujah>   and feeling   my feelings

did you see that the eleven Arizona electors voted as they were
expected to

also today   my friend lost a baby   and I am
                 weird and weeping   in love   with this horrible world
that makes women and holds them   in these bounded places

"To a Desert Poet" is the title of a broadside over this little desk

       My little desk of a heart
                              is broken

I used to promise to not make people laugh though no one asked
this of me

My best friend had a miscarriage

I wish the electors could

    What

I don't   know anymore
    "Of the beautiful and the felt" this poem says to me
from over the desk

        My felted heart moves slowly
    around this world

Unfathomable as it is, the world is not

this world is not

We got

       the president we deserve

Jane Miller told me to move to the desert to write my poems, the best place to be a poet

She imagined   for me   a life of more ease   expanse   than I have

I have   two jobs and still don't work as much as a lot of these fucking broken millennials

No more student debt   no more blaming screens for our grief
No more women's grief
No more queer grief   There are still people who subscribe

to lyricism and they are indeed / better poets than I am / you

know that feeling when you're making a salad in someone else's

house and you hear a Stevie Wonder song you'd never heard

before / and you feel like you're in an episode of *Scandal* and also

possibly in the last moment of your own life / I do want to be

listening to Stevie Wonder when I die / if at all possible / Right

now it's the Joy inside
my Tears inside my Pain inside my

I'm not sure what I aspire to
when it comes to the lyric

Is it the joy inside my painbody or is it the pain inside
my joybody   I think this apartment might be haunted

There is a ghost here   and she wears my glasses while I sleep

Then I wake up and read
Anne Carson: a deep green dream room

Alice Notley had never heard a Leonard Cohen song until he died

A small person saying "don't see me" when she doesn't want us
to look at her   she is crying
Today has been described as peak 2016

          All kinds of grief

What will "peak 2016" mean in 2017, 2018, 2019, 2020,
          Years I will need to see to believe

In 2008 I put a Barack Obama campaign sticker
          on a bottle of champagne
It felt like pushing my luck   until it was time to drink it
In 2016 I put a Hillary Clinton
campaign sticker on a bottle of champagne

and one night carried it with me in a green backpack from spot to
spot in Tucson it got warmer
and warmer
as the night went on and I still haven't opened it it's on my desk,
getting warmer as we dip into

summer 2017
I can't believe
          we made it out of the 20th century alive. I can't believe

  any of it   I need to strike

    the right balance. Need to remember to eat, drink water.

Yesterday I did not type anything but I did sew two lines through
a piece of paper and then drew an owl in crayon and sharpie. I
can't believe

we made it out of the early 2000s, the naughts, alive. I can't

believe all those times
     we crossed the street   or merged onto the highway

or went into the woods or

    onto a mountain you and me   you who had
a miscarriage   and the falling into creeks and cold wet clothes
but still   here we are   we

are here and it is 2017 and I can't believe we are alive it all seems

     so accidental but of course it is   an endlessly complex
system.

WE ARE DOWN HERE

"videos of world leaders crying"
– Olive Blackburn, *Communism is up there and we are down here but it is happening now*

1

The first amendment was an experiment
The second amendment was an experiment
The third amendment was an experiment
I don't know the whole
Bill of Rights it was an
experiment the seventh amendment
was an experiment

We talked a lot about a lot of it

I became the "we" when my grandparents
got their papers I am now liable
for all the experiments
"Well I'm not from here" is
some blood quantum shit I am
sorry for it all as if it was my

own personal decision // I have made
so many bad decisions it could easily have been
mine & now I have to fix it // we do //
I am the "we" that did this

2

I kept trying to quit my job kept saying I'm on my way out kept
acting badly theoretically
in the name of the collective
instead of leaving I got promoted and promoted and
promoted this is

whiteness // my general competency means I am now In Charge
my colleagues have called it magic my ability
to get promotions but it is just that I am white and always ready to leave
fucking Arizona

3

Joe Arpaio was convicted for ignoring a court's orders
that he was in violation of the
Bill of Rights the fourth amendment *The right of the people to be*

secure in their persons, houses, papers, and effects, against
unreasonable searches and seizures, shall not be violated, and no
Warrants shall issue, but upon probable cause, supported by Oath
or affirmation, and particularly describing the place to be searched,
and the persons or things to be seized.

LITERALLY NOTHING

My name is Hannah and I am a white queer poet and a subjective
entity and the literary director of a major U.S. American arts
organization I have

a brokerage account and yes I have
accepted below my market value and it was a privilege
to do that work but not in the way my employer tried to tell me
it was / he meant "an honor" and I meant "I could never do this job if
not for my fiscal emotional

familial and racialized safety net" I meant
"we are surrounded
by white U.S. Americans with advanced degrees who were born into
our shared socioeconomic class" I went to very good

public schools my whole life another
privilege though one cannot count them like 1 2 3 4 I also went

to a very mediocre public school where I earned a terminal degree
and they
paid me to do it / that piece of paper corresponds to such
ridiculously little work I can hardly
believe it / a lot of emotional work but other than that

recently I applied for a very coveted dream job and was offered it I
was a dream
candidate I was somehow overqualified
for it I am / literally nothing / special / a frog

in a bog / dozens of people in any room of 50 are more
intellectually physically spiritually emotionally astounding
than I am I am just a person who's had a lot this whole fucking time
I am
thirty years old thirty-one in

October

THINKPIECE, JULY 2017

Because I spend any time at all wondering what Oprah loves
I   also count my minutes   each one corresponding with x
number of dollars this hourly wage means that my

procrastination is me   stealing from myself I am deep
into this capitalism mindset   bodyset I sit   in my chair
for so many hours   I remember the thinkpieces

about how sitting   is killing
us is it   a thinkpiece if it is a scientific study
yes   but only if the scientific study is rendered

incompletely   people on the internet are saying you can't
have children anymore unless you want the environment to
be ruined   seems racist   seems corporate apologist   people
calling it   neoliberal   and they're right   that's 2017   for you

BEING WHITE WATCHING *FRIENDS*

1

The reason to rewatch television shows
that you've seen many times
is that it gets to be invisible
there in the background

In my poem about Madonna
Madonna gets to be invisible,
un-raced, white and/or nothing at all
In my poem about Madonna I too
considered myself racially invisible

Being white watching *Friends*
race is invisible for hours and hours
at a time

Being white watching basketball
I'm relieved when the commentators
call Kevin Love (white) a horse

but it's not actually a good sign
just that we've coded basketball successfully, that he's
successfully become a basketball body

2

It's not that Billy Collins is a Bad Guy, it's that
he believes himself to be a kind of invisible that demands
the superimposition of a visible film over himself for added
interest, e.g. a Chinese context. I have suffered from this too,
along with other lazy racialized poetics. I think we white poets
could practice
some radical compassion. Not forgiveness / not persona / not
striving for proximity but instead active apology and considering
our own racialized experiences /   positions / I would understand

if my childhood home needed to be seized
to make reparations happen.
It's not to say I would just shrug and say, "oh well,"
but it isn't actually amends
if it's easy. I don't have a house of my own,
so what do I have. The reason to rewatch
a television show with your parents is to watch them watching it
and to then be mad at them for being so much like you, like fear-you,
none of you a bad person. We have to let it be. There's an episode
of *Friends* where Monica makes birthday flan, and the other friends
don't like it, aren't excited to eat it, watching it we interject "racist"
at every flan joke. Part of it is that the 90s
sucked, though we love them, miss them, why is this
supposed to be funny, did white people not like custard in the 90s?
It's not that *Friends* is a Bad Show, it's that, in 2017, the task
is to speak something into the show that's not there, into a past self
that watched this show and noticed nothing at all the matter.

ON VACATION I CONTEMPLATE WORK AND DRAW SHEEP

"He was dictating a letter: *The goods about which you have inquired are the best of their kind made in the—*" when suddenly he stopped without completing the phrase. He looked at his secretary for a long time, and she looked at him until they both grew pale. Then he said, ... *'I have been wading in a long river and my feet are wet.'* He went out of the office for the last time and starting walking eastward toward Cleveland along a railroad track."
— introduction to Sherwood Anderson's *Winesburg, Ohio*

All of a sudden my human self obsessed with what the sheep's bleat "means" / if my human self met my poem self / well we wouldn't at all be surprised / in order to be in a place / to really feel in it / I need some quiet / I know there are other ways / ways other people feel present / so I try to help by / discussing too / processing aloud // the sheep / and emotional labor / do they do it / too / is grass on a mountain, moss-like in its carpeting, a fallacy / is my resistance to sharing a laugh / giving eye contact freely / a human quality / am I Wallace Stevens / a jerk in my day job / Sherwood Anderson / trailing off and walking out on my secretary mid-dictation / walking to Cleveland / and never coming back // as an introvert I am glad I do not have to dictate / my correspondence / my private thoughts aren't / all that bad / that's not quite it / when you're stuck for a solution // bleat it out / or don't / actually, most of these sheep are not bleating / there are probably sixty sheep here / and only four or five bleaters // too real / the activity of chewing / translated to their representative squiggle marks in my sketch // I had vivid enough dreams / but have forgotten them / when I woke up 9 hours ahead of the U.S. / I had to email directions to our dog sitter /

how to prepare food for our dog who has no pancreas to speak of / "pre-digest it, mama sheep," I should have said / leaving it at that

SHEEP POEM TWO

   Even now I'm thinking   this vacation will somehow change
me   that I will not click back into old routines   I will be Iceland
Hannah   this is the myth   of vacation that you can   continue
to look out the window   at sheep as they paw   at the grass
with their mamas

   By the car there are both   sleepy cows and cows running
joyously   my cousin Nitza's stories   about going on bus tours
with her then young daughter   who was disappointed that she
couldn't   see all the wild animals   that the others on the bus
could see   Nitza would point and say   "*Look, Na'ama, wild
cows!*"   this is mother love   mother care   the little lambs'
heads

butting their mamas' teats   for milk   we're not metaphors
we're animals   our human selves   changing   "*Don't forget the
happy thoughts   All it takes is happy thoughts*"   dozens and
dozens of waterfalls here

               dozens and dozens of sheep   cataracts pouring
down from a glacier   yes from a glacier but as if from nowhere
flow under the roads   we're on

I CANNOT BE CONSOLED

I had forgotten which exile
sadness was. I had wanted

to get it entirely. Watch

as I implement an idea:
many hands drowning

as if in a pond; descent

into a hole. If John Travolta
is in this room, he is being

quiet. Sadness is an exile.

I cannot be consoled. It is bad,
I mean good, to love a boy. He

is an emotion: I am feeling Travolta

today and I cannot be consoled.
I descend. I had wanted

to be a man but not everything

could be chosen. I must have entirely
forgotten his pretty face.

Watch: my bra, the sunset

draining over the party store. I tried
something and I cannot be consoled.

ECONOMY

Once, LeBron James was eighteen.   2003
In 2003, I was in high school, sixteen still in the summer.
In 2016, four-hundred forty-one NBA Summer League players   441—50
were competing for fifty NBA contracts.   11.3%, appx 1 in 9
Summer league players receive
a per diem, no salary, and sign an injury waiver $127.00/day
not to sue the NBA if they get hurt forever.
The NBA minimum salary for first-year players
as of the 2017-18 season is $815,615.   ≥ $815,615.00/yr
I played basketball from probably fifth grade to eighth, if that.   ~1995-98
Our team wore purple t-shirts, mine was way too big and one time
I made a three and in celebration shuffled backwards down the court
in my Penny One shoes. There was no reason for me to have shot   1¢
that three, if I remember correctly, I just did it. I hate capitalism
but I want another pair of Penny Ones. By contemporary standards   1¢
they're truly ugly, but you can get the reissued nostalgia shoe
for $59 + S/H if like me you can fit into boys' size   5.5 boys'
shoes. I'd like to read an essay titled
I PLAYED ON A SUMMER LEAGUE TEAM WITH LEBRON JAMES,
and I'd want it to be written by someone undrafted
who played in a Cleveland uniform with LeBron James
in the summer of 2003, maybe someone who tossed up one
of many 2003 Summer League alley-oops that LeBron received
and did impressive things with, someone who ultimately never signed $0.00/yr
an NBA contract. I'd want it to be about what he's up to now,
and what it was like to be eighteen on a basketball court,   2003
wanting so much, next to LeBron James.

AUGUST 11, 2016

I had a dream I forgot to vote "down ballot."
NPR talking about Gary Johnson

reminded me. When I fell to my knees
to request a second ballot

I didn't get felt tip I got a pencil & a ballpoint
& it turns out the questions I'd missed

were employee training manual meets
ethics test meets logic puzzle. Some

behavior/best practices stuff.
I still don't know the role of a private citizen.

I always feel weird about August.
Sometimes we do a controlled burn.

I'm sitting in the parking lot
of a Planet Fitness.

LOVE DREAM

LOVE DREAM

In the dream, Mary Kate and
Ashley and I were ecoterrorists
infiltrating corporate living.

Somewhere in or around LA
there were whole towns where
employees of chains would live

together. The homes looked like
giant restaurants and were
called things like I HEART

DAYS INN. Every dormitory
slathered with advertisements,
you could tell it was

like a cult, something
really creepy. Either Mary Kate
or Ashley was my partner,

but not the one that had
originally had a crush on me,
something like fifteen years

earlier. I waited in the car
for the one who gave me
the reddish hot chocolate mix I kept

on my dash in a Ziploc. My phone
wouldn't charge, and it was
because I hadn't plugged in

the other end. The one who had
originally had a crush on me
was breaking up with her husband

in another car, all the cars
were American cars. Doors slammed.
My partner was back, either

Mary Kate or Ashley. I loved
her in the dream, but knew
it was going to be a difficult time.

BREATH

I left the biggest space for it.

Have a hard time
thinking of it. Oh, it's supposed to be
so deep, go all the way down. *Breathe into your pelvis,*
into your feet. There comes a point

when you see that none of it is bullshit after all & at that point
no one wants to read your poems anymore. I probably peaked

at twenty-two. The universe is a breath
& every breath a universe. Oh, I've done it again:

took too big a breath, bigger than "natural." Told my girlfriend
I wasn't sighing at her. No longer a teenager. She's good; she
gets it.

The thing that got me hooked at first on breath
is how much warmer it is coming out than going in.

ME TOWN

There is a town where many of me live.
We all spell our name differently, and some of us say it differently,

but we are all me.
It is a happy town. Its citizens are all me. We spend our lives
avoiding suffering.

Suffering Is Not Inevitable is our town slogan and our fight song.
We put it on bumper stickers and sing it
when we play neighboring towns in basketball.

We yell it when we win, and we yell it too when we lose.
There is no church on Sundays, because everyone is Jewish.

Everyone is me.

In this town, there is a chamber ensemble
that performs in the band shell on Thursday nights
when it is not raining, we play *Suffering Is Not Inevitable* on
tuned idiophones
for those of us who are not watching television
or making a quiet dinner at home.

In this town, we all spend our lives avoiding suffering.
It is a happy town.

ANOTHER FEW CONSIDERATIONS

I do not like much
of the great literature. There are basic facts

of my personal history
that I still cannot account for.
When I meditate and sometimes

when I am falling asleep I attain a globular aspect and everything
becomes a basketball

with my consciousness floating
inches or miles or years above and I am touching it lightly with
the surfaces of my hands. Yesterday

getting out of my car I opened my door and almost killed Bob
who was on a bike and next to whom I used to meditate.

His bright yellow helmet. He was very nice about it.

At times I try to squeeze a blanket
or my knees to remind myself

where I am and how big
exactly. This always fails.

I am sure that it is me and not scale that is incorrect.

SOMETHING NOT NOTHING

A lie holds us hostage in ourselves. A hostage holds a knife but doesn't tell anyone because it will come in handy. A knife is an alibi. I was that, for a moment: calm, in a place. Breathing is a hinge and will come in handy. Breathing and being present are two elements of everything. History holds us to nothing in particular if we don't want it to. The word "remember" is a cultural icon. We do what we want. You are my hostage, you have a knife. A knife is a thing with feathers. A bird is falling out of the sky. The sky is a bird. I am a ship. The kitchen is on fire and full of water. My kitchen is full of water and not on fire. History is full of mistakes. Two mistakes diverge in a wood. A floating head in a swimming pool is unexpected. Surprise is terror. Surprise is terror. Terror is jubilation. All emotions are one emotion. How are you? All emotion is one emotion. Monotony is excitement. Lighting the stove in the kitchen full of water is impossibility. Impossibility is an emotion is terror is glee. If your kitchen is on fire fill it with water. If your heart is aflame you have a problem. A problem is a bird that cannot fly e.g. a penguin e.g. a chicken. A chicken is a bird we eat. Another bird we eat is hope. Chickens and hope in a kitchen full of water, aflame on the stove. A stove is a city, a city is Boston, Boston is a state, a state is another large metropolis. Aren't we all metropoles? No. I am a stove full of water. I am a ship.

HARBAUGH IN APRIL

These poems don't have
the head of Jim Harbaugh
floating around in them.
We are the intangibles
everyone's been talking about.
We ask can a sporting event
dismantle hegemony . . . and if
not the game then the activity
around the game . . . queer as shit:
Russell Westbrook. Queer eyes
on the straight guy. We are the lines
drawn onto and around
the action. The players now
chess pieces, profit margins,
props. Bodies, bro. Apparel holders:
mannequins. When what I think I want
is tattoos what I really want is:
those arms. The whistle
blows the play dead. Someone else
always deciding fact.

U.S. SOMATIC

1.

When hot ketchup drips off a burger
& onto your finger

try considering it "touch"

You may have to begin
by closing your eyes
but ultimately

after a lot of practice

you may be able to do this wakefully

2.

Eat the fries

knowing
they are
fatty

and bad for America
you are bad

for America too this is a country
full

of bad for itself

I SEND SEXY TEXTS WITH ATHLETES

The new TV is smaller than the old TV but better. Cords connect all the parts to each other. One end the male end but only one. Mirrors I've been told open up small spaces. I set up the mirrors by the TV and end up watching myself watching TV. I can see already how this could become bad for me. *It is the task of a lifetime,* she says, *avoiding boredom.* Yesterday while breathing my inhale was grace and my exhale confidence. I am on the sixth season of several TV shows and I have gone through all the emotions with them: they were TV emotions: some more than others. I have been told there is no separate self. I am wide-eyed watching this. I am going to leave this room and never come back to it.

BASQUIAT

Surprised   when people haven't heard of him. The ques-
amazed
not surprised   tion of what work is real, people asked that

of Basquiat. Erased him as he erased words of his own. He died;

most of us do. He painted money that became real. Kevin Young

calls it alchemical. More people should get money that way. Better

than none at all. More often than not I put "art" in quotation marks

because of having taken it "too" seriously. Putting something in

quotation marks is not crossing it out, is more a bracketing. A

different attention-getting mechanism, different histories. I am a

"simple" "artist." I hope we make potato prints. All this philosophical

shaking and prodding we need: I'm only just seeing it now. Levity!

Levity! All this thinking about pain. I'll show you pain! Just kidding.

I won't.

PORTAL

The nonsense graphics of television promos
for sports that men play on TV

Like what is that? Gears and transformers
and metal sounds and a sudden basketball court with what seems
maybe to be
PVC pipes and

masculinity in its abstract workings

I love a quick lead from Utah
I love knowing as little about the Pac-12 as I know six years into
living in Tucson
I love eating fries, drinking wine, reading Proxies, and basketball on

I dream of turning off the commentators and listening instead to
Joan Osborne's "One of Us"
on repeat
changing the channel turning off those commentators too

watching Kyrie Irving bob & float & almost fall over & make another
off-balance shot with seconds on the clock while Joan says *yeah,
yeah*, and

while I like this dreamed up combination taking hold instead of the
commentators' constant talking, implying that athletes are god-like is
another more complimentary but still very real version of spectatorial
structural racism

And anyway I'm not listening to "One of Us," and the Cavs are not on
nor is the sound in this bar
When it comes to what we should do about, it I am a proponent of
keep getting them checks

Give the athletes all their money. All the profits. And

yeah, I wonder about Joan Osborne, looking her up on IMDB to see if she's had any TV or film cameos, wonder what the odds are that she and Kyrie would show up in a commercial together

Joan Osborne, July 8, RULED BY THE MOON, THIS ASTROLOGICAL SIGN IS ALL ABOUT FEELINGS, EMOTIONS, IMAGINATION, AND CREATIVITY. Kyrie Irving, March 23, ARIES WITH MARS AS ITS RULER REPRESENTS COURAGE, STRENGTH, INDEPENDENCE, COMPETITION, AND ENTHUSIASM.

POSTCARD, LAUNDROMAT CAFÉ, REYKJAVIK ICELAND

Is it really ten o'clock? I am sitting here next to
two plastic bags of my still-damp clothes
feeling ready for bed. This drawer of notes,
missives from the past, from people
who can drink a lot more than I can. Yesterday
a reporter asked LeBron James if it was important
to defend home court (to win games 3 and 4
in Cleveland—down two games to the Warriors
like last year) and in response he said, "Are you
a smart man?" Today, we saw a lot of art
by a smart man. We are here for a conference
at the university. Iceland's president
addressed us. Former university professor, professor
of history, author of true books. As a rule,
I don't bet against LeBron James, because he has
a photographic memory; is a very smart man.

ACUPUNCTURE, A PRACTICE

I thought I was thinking but does thinking require the engagement of long-term memory? I thought I was thinking but I think I was asleep. I had patterned myself to believe my body would think for me there. Tell me more about Oolong tea. A woman I know is ill and goes to the tea house; the woman there loves her like I do. Both women love their acupuncturists. I've been asking everyone

if they go to acupuncture. My tea has probably steeped long enough. To be the studied object (e.g. of a dissertation, a short book): it is bound to forge a friendship, a sister.

MOVE TO TUCSON

In Tucson at the right time
a train goes by / Monday
in the middle of the day too late

for coffee but you are having coffee
by the train tracks / the man who enters

the coffee shop is wearing
that shirt you always
wanted / and you

short hair woman you are

in a coffee shop your
own short hair woman
as you always wanted to be

In Tucson in the coffee shop
the men mostly do not

talk   *Move to Tucson*   the men mostly
are quiet in the coffee shop except

how is your band
doing / Flagstaff and Phoenix and Flagstaff
and Phoenix / There's seven of us
now / at the ballroom

you are not romantically interested
in any of the men
in the coffee shop your relation

to desire and the men is much
more nuanced than romance it is
related to t-shirts you are

your own short hair lover your own
woman your own short hair
in the coffee shop

the one where the men mostly do not talk and the windows
show the train   *Move to Tucson*   as it rattles by and is gone

ANOTHER STORY ABOUT THE SAME TRAINS

Every story about photographic history follows the same line drawn. The same three names in the same paragraph followed by January 7, 1839. I know this book is going to say pyramids before it does. I haven't backed up my computer in 259 days and I am reading about the annihilation of space and time. When I used to read I would do it with a notebook and a task. Now the task is vague and I do not know where my notebook is. I have probably read this page before, likely two or three times. I wrote a poem eight years ago with what in retrospect seems a quaint detail and indeed was invented to be so at the moment by its narrative-builders: Joe Biden on a train.

"The day that Hillary conceded the 2008 primaries, I rode the train back from Washington to New York with another political journalist." So much has happened in eight years. We are nine days from the 2016 presidential election. If I was your mother I would suggest a ride on the rails or getting out of Tucson. Around the corner, signs about Crooked Hillary and we might as well be in another moment, I wish we were and I'm glad we're not. Technology accelerating the moment. I am terrified and unconvinced that I should be otherwise.

THERE'S AN OLD SAYING: A COVER

Love me once, shame on

Shame on you.

Love me
You can't get loved again.

LOVE DREAM

A man and a woman stretch in a courtyard.
I am looking at a photograph of them. You are too.
You point out that it's not a man

and a woman, but that one of them is a young dolphin.
You point, and I see what you mean. I say, "Thank you,"
and think, "That one isn't even a woman: it's a goat."

I can't believe you didn't notice. There are four shadows
on the wall where I have hung the photograph. The shadow
that overlaps with the picture frame moves

in a way I don't notice. Even when this day is over,
and the shadow is gone, we will still be in Detroit. And so will
the photograph. In which the goat helps the child dolphin stretch.

You and I look at the photograph for a minute. I say something
to you that you like. Then we're doing something else. I love you.

SPECTACULAR 06: AMERICA'S NEXT TOP MODEL

When I think back on our relationship, I think about the time we watched that episode of *America's Next Top Model* where Tyra makes Nicole and Jayla think they've been eliminated, but then she yells BECAUSE WE'RE ALL GOING TO LONDON!! and there's confetti everywhere and Nicole makes a face like she's been violated, like somebody violated her, and suddenly there's a Union Jack in the shot and Tyra wraps it around her hips and struts around like that and Nicole cries and cries.

SPECTACULAR 07: *FRIENDS*, 1994

Sometimes an episode of *Friends* comes on and I feel like I got in a time machine. The boys' apartment is filled with fruit baskets because Joey is so good at sex. Monica is frantic at Rachel. This is the season finale, which I know because Rachel can't stop thinking about Ross and about kissing Ross but Ross is about to get off a plane with Julie. He is dating Julie, which we can tell by the way they hold hands and kiss in the breezeway. We're not to that scene yet, but I remember it from the last several times I watched this episode, plus the episode that happens after it when they play that part of this episode again. That's not exactly dramatic irony: my knowing. Here's what will happen: Flight 457 from Beijing will arrive. Rachel's head will start bleeding, and she'll try to fix it with flowers. Everyone will be watching, and Ross will yell RACHEL!! and then she will be more awkward than she's ever been and ever will be again, including that time in the seventh season when she gets really mad at Winona Ryder for claiming to have forgotten the time when the two of them made out in college.

A PROBLEM AND SOME SPACE

A girlfriend phoned me the other day and said come on over
nobody's home. I went over. Nobody was home.

Between what a girlfriend says and what I think: some space.
We have a problem

and some space, how wrong I can be: I am a wide-open peach
jar when a girlfriend phones me. I wouldn't be

insincere. During tv shows a girlfriend wants to braid my hair
but I prefer to keep my pants on. The guy on the tv: he's
singing

and it's good. I'm watching Letterman during sex. He doesn't
know I'm here but he's doing great. I am peaches and the
basket. I am

the person who picks the peaches, pits 'em, eats 'em, when a
girlfriend phones. During sex

a girlfriend always wants to talk to me. Just the other night she
called me from a hotel.

ONEONTA, NY

A poem with | a place as its | title should
exhaust | the place or drown | the reader
in what it is | to be there | in that place.
Alternately it could be | an ode to a woman
who lives there | or lived | there or
who said | the place name | in an
appealing way | over coffee. | But too
many poems | are for | women. I don't
even know any, | not anymore. | Have
you been to 2013? | It is | a very new place.

HOROSCOPE FOR HUMANITY, JULY 2017

It is 8 pm on a Sunday, and I have set a meditation timer on YouTube. The delicate bells are there to remind me to wake up into this span. To write a truly awake poem for humanity. To humanity, I offer this: it is time for a power grab. I suggest: the problems are not what we think the problems are; there are other problems. For three minutes every Sunday night at 8 pm, ring a bell for when doing nothing is not enough. Ring a bell for your sister. Ring a bell for your mother. Ring a bell for mothers. Ring a bell for the pain of the mother, look at photographs of the Pietá and let yourself feel all the feelings that arise for the mothers who have or wield pain in one way or another. For the mother or the mother-in-law of your mother who hurts. When the bell rings remember yourself as mother, whether or not fertility is immediately present in your way of being in the world. There is no feminine version of many words but I suggest we make one. I would suggest a power grab. I would suggest arming yourself. It is 8 pm on a Sunday, any Sunday, and I am setting a meditation timer to write a truly awake poem. All my dogs are sleeping. All my friends are weaving. CA Conrad is slowing down their evening, 8 pm on a Sunday in July, in order to wake up in the morning and check the drone deaths from the 24 hours that we are part of right now. Right now is a way to be awake. I would suggest a power grab. I would suggest being the kombucha mother. I would suggest fecundity and drinking plutonium water, lead water, poison, in this world. I would suggest watching a dog sleep for the duration of her sleep, for the duration of his sleep. I would suggest being an empath about her cheek on the blanket, his cheek on the cot. I would suggest arming yourself with study. I would suggest heavy use of the library. I would suggest a power grab, being the 11% who believe you should recognize, identify, and pursue what is yours. You have more vision than you allow. Be your own vision. Be your own woven cloth. Be a wrinkled cheek, nap-deep, on the cot. I have an article to recommend. This is my horoscope for humanity.

SPECTACULAR 08: NEW YEAR'S EVE 2011/2012

It's New Year's Eve, and I'm watching Anderson Cooper and Kathy Griffin play-bicker like you and I would if we hadn't had sex. They giggle

a lot, and Kathy Griffin is threatening to disclose things that she and Anderson Cooper talk about off-camera. She mostly hints, and I am riveted: she slips a little out: last year on New Year's Eve, for instance,

they went back to Kathy Griffin's hotel room and drank. They might have played cards. If this year is any indication of how last year went, they got sillier and sillier as the night went on. Anderson Cooper looks pretty uncomfortable and shocked and happy, and I'm pretty sure Anderson

Cooper and Kathy Griffin have never so much as made out, I'm pretty sure it's something else.

OPENING LINES OF MOBY DICK: A COVER

I used to read on a different plane. Now I'm Jane the Virgin.
Watching TV or when my sister visits: this is my substitute for
pistol and ball. When I get to knocking a bunch of idiots' dumb
poet hats off their pretentious heads, I know that I'm totally
PMSing.

VULVAS IN THE ACADEMY

There was a CFP
about vulva-touching
I responded
I said I am currently
touching my vulva
I was accepted
to the conference
when I showed up
I had no vulva
I said gotcha
I said *what is a vulva*
to you
they said
are you still touching your vulva
that was their answer
I couldn't believe it
I went home
without attending
any of the other panels

WALLACE STEVENS'S "POEMS OF OUR CLIMATE": A COVER

Nothing is ever perfect

& we get off on that.
It's erotic: how bad

I am at loving.

MEMORY: CONNECTICUT, 2012

16. Things That Make One's Heart Beat Faster

All summer I thought that writing about Joe Paterno was what I needed to be doing. I bought Café Bustelo in the yellow can because it was $3 for that whole can, and it didn't taste too bad. The shopping I did was at Walmart, which I convinced myself was the only choice. Ah, the need for pleasure and what my mother calls "retail therapy"! I have brought both back to the desert. On the first page of *Moby Dick,* Ishmael says THIS IS MY SUBSTITUTE FOR PISTOL AND BALL, it is my favorite line in all of literature. I have a new therapist today. It is 2012 and I am drinking whiskey out of a glass my boyfriend calls the goblet of fire. It is mostly just a normal glass, but calling it this makes us both happy. All summer I wore a LeBron James jersey in public. I rode my bike even though there was no reason for it.

17. Things That Arouse a Fond Memory of the Past

I did not fix my broken air conditioning, and the highway became intolerable. So many times I would sweat all the way to New Haven. There was a bar called Tata's that had mofongo. I only went to the ocean once: a mistake. The whole thing was. All summer I neglected plants that were under my charge. My needs too were ignored, but I did not metaphorize the dead plants; my life was separate from theirs. All summer there was a way of living, and I couldn't get to it. Or what is more likely, I was in it and living it, and it just felt the worst.

19. Oxen Should Have Very Small Foreheads

All summer I was in the same time zone as my parents for once and still didn't call them. I was in the same region as my aunt and uncle for once and still didn't see them. All summer I sat at one table in the cafeteria I sat there every day very conspicuously. I sat there every day very conspicuously. I sat there all the time except when I went instead to get margaritas and tacos in the middle of the fucking day. I would talk to the bartender about Kobe and the Lakers. Steve Nash. After that I would day-nap. Too long. All summer I ate Heath Bar-flavored Klondike bars because they were in the freezer and I felt awful when I wasn't eating them. This summer there was no me so it makes sense that I alienated my loved ones. They loved a thing that was gone: it was like how I felt when there were no more Heath Klondikes. I'm not trying to be cute I'm trying to be accurate.

80. Things That Have Lost Their Power

This summer I went to a Redbox for the first time. It was at a Walgreens slightly to the west but I needed support so I took a friend who was also sad. And then the second time I picked movies that only I wanted to see without consulting with anyone. I could stand to remember that I can pick what I want. Tonight it is 2012 and I'm looking forward to a Snickers ice cream bar that I probably won't even get. I am sitting here in boxers stamped *ESPN ESPN ESPN ESPN ESPN ESPN.* If I sit like this with my legs apart you can't see my vulva because fabric is in the way. But if I put my legs together it is less certain that fabric will obscure that part of me. This seems a grand irony. All summer I did not think enough about being ladylike. I joked that I was going to wear a tie to the final banquet and then I did.

A HUMBLE SEE

Today, in the middle of May, I was irritated.
It will not make me die. A fluctuation

calling itself Oliver
pointed me upwards where it saw birds
but not me, it could name them not me. Birds

in the closet of the sky, hope way up there I fail to hope,
all the things on the beach. Several.

When in doubt, Oliver said,
consider the possibility that beauty is not here for us. "Not." I
cannot sleep

at a sheared-off cliff, and I cannot rise
above it either, it a cliff and I a human no bird.
Three paychecks later and still

no bird. Still the birds
are somewhere I cannot see, maybe not
the same birds but still.

ACKNOWLEDGEMENTS

Versions of some of these poems have appeared online and in print; thanks to the following venues and the publishers behind each: *PEN Poetry Series, Spork Press, Denver Quarterly, Bat City Review, CutBank, JUPITER88, Split Lip, Evening Will Come, Apartment Poetry, The Feminist Wire, and Crab Orchard Review.*

Additionally, a few personal thanks are due.

Thank you to my teachers, guides, mentors: Keith Taylor, Jane Miller, Laura Kasischke, Leslie Stainton, Anne Carson and Robert Currie, Ander Monson, and Alison Hawthorne Deming. Additional early readers of this manuscript helped move it elsewhere: Kristi Maxwell, Brian Blanchfield, and Eileen Myles, thank you.

To my family: figuring out what it means to be an Ensor, a Wolfe, a Karmel, a Brown, is the whole thing. You give me a lot to lean into, and I love you. This book is in honor of my remarkable Nana, Elizabeth Brown Ensor, who writes me poems to this day; and in memory of my grandmother and great-aunt, Henia Karmel Wolfe and Ilona Karmel, who I wish I had a proper chance to impress and infuriate.

To my family: TC Tolbert, the brilliant-hearted, I wouldn't have written half the shit in here if it weren't for you making opportunities for me to stretch toward and insisting that I do it. Kristen E. Nelson, you are truly my home. Elizabeth Frankie Karamazov Rollins, magician, curiosity, ever picking tiny spines out of my sweatshirt. You three make the space. I'm in it.

Oh, Audra Puchalski, my poem life partner. Laura Wetherington, collaborator in feel pieces and slow feeling. I'll see you two at the Old Town. Biggest hugs too to Shaelyn Smith, Jeff Ham, Anna Ash, Claire Sylvester Smith, and Marie Sweetman. Thanks to my 514 beloveds with a sunny porch sit of gratitude to Olga Semenova. To the New England Literature Program (all four iterations of yous), with special thanks to Rachael Cohen.

Most of this book was written on the traditional homeland of the Tohono O'Odham nation, where I lived without ever having asked. The desert and its community stay with me, and I owe more than my gratitude.

Since this is my Tucson book, thanks to everyone there for their joy, conversation, alchemy, and generosity. The list is longer, but here's a start: Lisa O'Neill, Kimi Eisele, John Melillo, Annie Guthrie, Lori Van Buggenum, Samuel Ace, Johanna Skibsrud, Beth Alvarado, Rosalind Perera, Ian Ellasante, Debbie Weingarten, Arianne Zwartjes, Steve Salmoni, Riley Beck Iosca, Frank Jude Boccio, Susan Briante, Farid Matuk, Lisa Strid, Jessica Langan-Peck, Cory Aaland, and Meg Wade. Thanks too, of course and always, to Casa Libre en la Solana and the University of Arizona Poetry Center. Oh, and for changing my cells (my ancestors and I thank you): Logan Byers, Azrael Avey Nim, Cielo Quetzal, Barbara Bancroft, and Michelle Marks.

Thank you to Tyler Meier, who gave me a job and widened the margins, deepened the conversation. Consider me on call, boss. Ditto you, Natalie Diaz.

A deep bow and thank you to my love, Aisha Sabatini Sloan, whose endless creative vision and heart space has made living/writing/being pivot.

And finally, endless gratitude to Suzi F. Garcia and Carmen Giménez Smith, heroes both, for picking this manuscript out of a pile and offering their vision, challenges, and questions to help me see it better, to make a book where once there was no book. Working with the two of you has been everything I've ever needed/wanted. And to my friend Sarah Gzemski, for putting up with me in so many of my most particular moments and modes, and still making this physical object happen, along with a million other things. Noemi Press is completely, 100%, for real.

NOTES

"DESIRE" p. 10 – The quotation in italics is from one of my favorite essays—Ross Gay's "No Pressure No Diamonds: Ross Gay, Hazel Meyer, and Shooting Out of the Phone Booth." The essay can be found at http://www.somecallitballin.com/no-pressure-no-diamonds-gay/.

"HAREM" p 12 and "AN AQUEDUCT" p 41 – These were written in collaboration / in process alongside Jill Darling and Laura Wetherington.

"ON TELEVISION IN POEMS" p 13 – See also Jane Miller, *A Palace of Pearls* (Copper Canyon, 2005).

"ON INSTANT REPLAY" p 35 – See also Tan Lin, *Seven Controlled Vocabularies and Obituary 2004. The Joy of Cooking: [AIRPORT NOVEL MUSICAL POEM PAINTING FILM PHOTO HALLUCINATION LANDSCAPE]* (Wesleyan University Press, 2010).

"GREEN AVENTURINE RELEASES OLD PATTERNS, HABITS, AND DISAPPOINTMENTS SO NEW GROWTH CAN TAKE PLACE" p 44 – This exact phrasing that serves as the title to this poem appears in many places, including but not limited to crystalvaults.com, newmoonbeginnings.com, orgoneartist.com, and everydayritualco.com. The quotation in lines 1-2 is from Chance the Rapper's "Summer Friends," and in lines 4-6 from Olive Blackburn's *Communism is up there and we are down here but it is happening now*.

"SPECTACULAR 05: RIGHT" – See Femi Omoni, "The Reframing of Black America: The Portrayal of African Americans in American Television Crime Dramas" (Masters thesis, April 2017, accessible online via Duke University Library website).

"U.S. SOMATIC" p 90 and "HOROSCOPE FOR HUMANITY, JULY 2017" p 106 – These owe a great deal to CA Conrad, both for (of COURSE) their somatic exercises and for the Naropa SWP workshop they led in June 2017 that primed me to come home and write this horoscope.